IMAGES
of Wales

CENTRAL CARDIFF

'A visitor to the modern and beautiful City of Cardiff will see a vastly different place to what I saw on my arrival in 1859, the main features of which had very little changed since they were pictured in Speed's map of 1610.'

Sam Allen, 1918

IMAGES
of Wales

CENTRAL CARDIFF

Compiled by
Brian Lee

For Bill Smith

Keen on lucking winners, Bill

All the best

Brian Lee

TEMPUS

First published 1998
Copyright © Brian Lee, 1998

Tempus Publishing Limited
The Mill, Brimscombe Port,
Stroud, Gloucestershire, GL5 2QG

ISBN 0 7524 1138 1

Typesetting and origination by
Tempus Publishing Limited
Printed in Great Britain by
Midway Clark Printing, Wiltshire

This book is dedicated to my daughter, Amanda, and my son-in-law, Russell

Contents

The Arms of Cardiff. The banner seen in the centre, supported by Cardiff's dragon, bears the arms of Iestyn ap Gwrgan, the last Welsh ruler of Morgannwg.

Foreword

Nothing evokes nostalgia quite like an old photograph. Suddenly the past comes alive before our eyes as we once again look at long-forgotten faces and places. In Cardiff particularly, there continues to be a real enthusiasm for the city's past. Perhaps we think of this interest in old Cardiff as being quite recent, but this is not really so. As early as the 1860s, residents of the town were commenting sadly on the rapid changes that were taking place, and at least one local artist found a ready market for his views of disappearing landmarks.

The coming of popular photography, 130 or so years ago, enabled us for the first time to accurately record the changing face of Cardiff. This wonderful legacy of old photographs and postcards provides us with fresh treasures, as they continue to surface from dusty drawers and albums.

Cardiffians all have particular memories of their own district, and the success of books from the *Archive Photographs* Series on Canton, Llandaff, Grangetown, Cathays and so forth, have brought enormous pleasure to so many residents both young and old. This book on Central Cardiff differs from these however, in that it represents our shared experiences, and our memories of 'town', where we all, at one time or another, had our first taste of big shops, of cafés, and of theatres. Even today, and despite its large size and population, Cardiff has something of the small town about it, a pleasant sense of intimacy and friendliness.

Standing at the heart of it all is Cardiff's oldest building, the Castle, which has witnessed nearly 2,000 years of history since it was first founded by invading Roman legions. Although the Castle is now taken for granted by most Cardiffians, it cannot be ignored, forming as it does a magnificent centrepiece to the city. It was not always so, and some senior residents may recall the early 1920s and before, when houses on both sides of Duke Street obscured the Castle. It is also hard to believe that at one time, grapevines grew up the Castle walls. Much credit is due to the late fourth Marquis of Bute, whose care ensured that the look and setting of the Castle was as appealing as it remains today.

The other great feature of the city is surely the Civic Centre, which includes some of the most magnificent Edwardian buildings in the country. It is exactly a century since the Corporation purchased Cathays Park from the Bute family for the purpose of building a new Town Hall. Shortly after its completion, this became the City Hall, as city status had been conferred in 1905. In the years that followed, other buildings appeared, including the National Museum of Wales, the University, and the Welsh Office. Photographs of this area chart its fascinating development throughout the present century.

But it is in Cardiff's commercial centre that we witness the greatest changes. High Street, St Mary Street and Queen Street, which sprung from the medieval street plan, are still the main thoroughfares today. However, it is fascinating to see familiar buildings suddenly looking quite different, in the days when the traffic was horse-drawn, and the pace of life, slower. Even images from the comparatively recent past show how swift the process of change is.

Our nostalgia for what has gone should not be too romantic. For some of the faces we see in these old photographs, life was one of toil, disease and discomfort. The 'Courts' of little houses, often built within sight of the opulent new department stores of James Howell and David Morgan, were picturesque, but they were also mean, filthy slums, without decent sanitation, lighting or heating.

How welcome the theatres, music halls and cinemas must have been, providing entertainment for all, in the days before radio and television. Other public amenities, such as the Old Library, and the Cory, Stuart and Park Halls, have either been altered, or have disappeared altogether. Likewise, the new Millennium Stadium is rising from the site of its predecessor, the Arms Park, and that of the Empire Pool, once again drastically changing the landscape.

Such is the way of progress, and Cardiff has always been a city of change. Its rapid expansion during the last century caused it to be once called 'the Welsh Chicago', and as it approaches the new millennium, a great regeneration is once more revitalizing the city. Cardiff is at last becoming a true capital, with a devolved National Assembly, an exciting new waterfront and a feeling of self confidence which evokes, just as these splendid photographs do, the spirit of a great commercial past.

Matthew Williams
Curator of Cardiff Castle
May 1998

One
Cardiff Castle

In 1883, Lord Bute gave orders that carved animal figures should be mounted on the wall of the Castle.

The Corner House, Cardiff Castle, *c.* 1876. It was demolished in 1877.

The Corner House with its bay window can also be seen in the centre of this picture, *c.* 1870.

The animal figures were moved to
their present site, west of the clock
tower, in 1928.

Cardiff trams took to the streets in 1902, around the time that this picture of Cardiff Castle was
taken.

The Chaucer Tower, *c*. 1920.

The third Marquis of Bute and his architect, William Burgess, rebuilt the south wing of the Castle in 1893.

12

The mound upon which the Keep stands was said to be the work of Danes, who had a settlement in the area during the tenth and eleventh centuries. However, it is more likely to be of Norman origin.

The West Gate, seen to the right of the picture, was rebuilt in 1921.

13

In 1115, the Earl (or Consul) of Gloucester, Lord of Cardiff Castle, is believed to have built the early stone keep as well as the great south wall and the wall on the west of the Castle. They were constructed on remaining Roman masonry.

In 1158, Cardiff Castle was taken by surprise and Robert Consul's son, William, was taken prisoner by Ivor Bach, the Welsh Lord of Senghenydd.

It was around 1423 that Richard Beauchamp, Earl of Warwick, built the central part of Cardiff Castle.

In 1404, in the reign of Henry IV, the Castle and town of Cardiff were almost entirely destroyed by Owen Glyndwr.

In 1776, Lord Bute set about putting the Castle in habitable repair. He began by pulling down the great wall, which connected the Black Tower, near the entrance, with the keep. The walls were so strong though that he had to use gunpowder.

The Library, Cardiff Castle, *c.* 1912.

The Dining Room, Cardiff Castle. The figures on the over-mantle represent the Old Testament story of Abraham and Sarah.

The fireplace and mantle in the
Banqueting Hall, Cardiff Castle, *c.* 1902.

A detail of a fireplace, in Cardiff Castle,
c. 1902.

Two
Civic Centre

An aerial view of Central Cardiff. The Civic Centre is to the top of the picture.

The Glamorganshire Canal was opened in 1794, as a means of transporting iron from Merthyr Tydfil to Cardiff Docks. The last barge passed down it in 1942. This picture was taken around 1906.

The Friary Gardens, which are sometimes mistakenly called Priory Gardens, *c.* 1948. The statue of the third Marquis of Bute was designed by Dr P. MacGillivray and was unveiled in 1930.

The Law Courts, *c*. 1950. The statue of Gwilym Williams of Miskin, Stipendiary Judge and Squire, can be seen to the right of the picture.

The City Hall was designed by Lanchester, Stewart and Rickards, who also designed the Law Courts. The South Africa War Memorial, which was the work of Albert Toft, can be seen under the dome of the City Hall, *c*. 1910.

Judge Gwilym Williams, (1839–1906). He was a King Edward VII lookalike, and his statue stands outside the Law Courts. 'The crowning glory of the man was his ardent love for his nation – its tradition, its people, its music, its poetry, its language, its life, which he touched with every facet.' (Sir Thomas Hughes, *Great Welshmen of Modern Days*)

The South Africa War Memorial was erected in memory of around 200 soldiers who were killed serving in Welsh regiments.

This statue of John Cory, the coal owner and philanthropist, was erected in 1906. This picture was taken around 1945.

Gorsedd Gardens, Cathays Park, *c.* 1936. 'In front of the National Museum is a flower garden, and on the green turf is a circle of rough unhewn stones, the Gorsedd Circle of the Bards of the Island of Britain.' – J. Kyrle Fletcher.

The National Museum of Wales. The foundation stone was laid in 1912, but owing to the First World War, the main block and western galleries were not opened until 1927. The statue is of Lord Ninian Crichton-Stuart MP, who was killed in the Battle of Loos, in 1915.

Glamorgan County Hall, *c.* 1950. The sculptured groups at either end of the steps symboliz[e] Navigation and Mining. The building was opened in 1912 and extended in 1932.

The National War Memorial of Wales standing in the centre of Alexandra Gardens, *c*. 1930. It was unveiled by Edward, Prince of Wales, on 12 June 1928.

CF 8   BOARD OF HEALTH BUILDING. CARDIFF

Alexandra Gardens, *c*. 1930. The statue to the left of the picture depicts Henry Austin Bruce, the first Lord of Aberdare and the first president of the University of Wales. The Board of Health building, now the Welsh Office, is in the background.

The Temple of Peace was erected as a gift to the Welsh people by the first Lord Davies of Llandinam. It was opened in 1938 by one of the bereaved mothers of the First World War.

The University College of Wales' west wing was opened in 1909, and the rest of the building was constructed between 1912 and 1962.

The Marble Hall, in City Hall.

A statue of Godfrey Charles Morgan, the first Viscount Lord Tredegar. His horse, Sir Briggs, carried him unscathed in the famous Charge of the Light Brigade at Balaclava. The statue was erected during his lifetime in 1909. Note the misspelling of Cathays on the top of the postcard.

A statue of Earl Lloyd George was erected in Gorsedd Gardens, in 1960. It was in the City
Hall's Marble Hall that Lloyd George received the freedom of the City of Cardiff and where he
delivered his great address in Welsh. This picture shows him with his wife and daughter
Megan.

Three
Streets and Buildings

Kingsway, *c.* 1950. The town pound was once situated near the gentlemen's toilet.

An important feature of old Cardiff was its town wall and gates. The North Gate stood on a site adjacent to the Rose & Crown public house, now called Cooper's, seen on the right of both pictures.

Legend has it that Duke Street was named after Robert, Duke of Normandy, who was imprisoned in Cardiff Castle in 1126. The earliest form of the name suggests an association with ducks or poulterers. The street was widened in 1924 and the row of shops abutting the castle wall was knocked down.

'... mid nineteenth-century Duke Street, formerly called Shoemaker Street, the shops and houses were of a whimsical architecture.' – from Sam Allen's *Reminiscences*.

Queen Street, in 1909.

Electric tramcars came to Cardiff, on 25 March 1902. Members of the Tramways Committee travelled from the Tramway Power Station, Newport Road, to St John's Square, *c.* 1909. The corner of Charles Street can be seen on the extreme left of the picture.

When this Queen Street picture was taken, around 1949, the days of the prototype double-deck covered tram were nearly at an end. On 20 February 1950, the last Cardiff tram made its final journey.

The Carlton Restaurant, Queen Street. This photograph was taken by Tony Lebeau in 1939, when he was an apprentice electrician. Note his workmate overhauling the electric lighting on the letter 'A' of Carlton. The restaurant was a popular venue for wining, dining and dancing, and was damaged by Nazi bombers in 1941. British Home Stores was later built on the site.

The offices seen in the centre of the picture in Dumfries Place, around 1950, have now been replaced with a multi-storey car park.

Queen Street, *c*. 1904.

Queen Street, *c.* 1949.

Spital Cottages, Crockherbtown, in 1883. The name Crockherbtown, dating from 1776, is thought to have originated from the fact that potherbs were cultivated by the monks of Greyfriars. In 1886, when the town council changed the name Crockherbtown to Queen Street, there were many objections, sadly all to no avail.

Old houses in St Mary Street. This picture was probably taken in 1896, when Cardiff staged the great Fine Art, Maritime and Industrial Exhibition.

The Great Western Hotel, in 1907. The statue of John, the second Marquis of Bute, was erected in front of the High Street Town Hall in 1853. Sculpted by I. Evan Thomas, it was moved to it present position in 1879.

When this statue stood in High Street, Kyrle Fletcher, in his *Cardiff Notes: Picturesque and Biographical*, had this to say, 'This Lord Bute has a full right to stand here and look up the street at his Castle entrance, for he was the maker of modern Cardiff.' Cardiff Bay Development Corporation has submitted plans to relocate the statue from the monument end of St Mary Street, to a location in Bute Street, in 1999.

The Terminus Hotel, on the right of the picture, is now sadly known as Sam's Bar.

The Wyndham Arcade was built around 1887, and can be seen in both these pictures of St Mary Street.

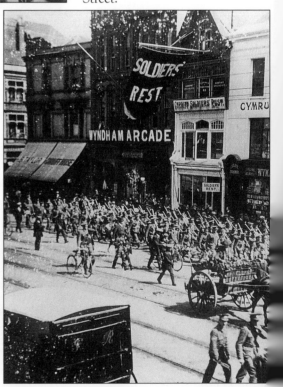

The Philharmonic, St Mary Street. Bunting was strung up for the visit of the Duke of Clarence, in 1890.

St Mary Street, *c.* 1905.

St Mary Street, *c.* 1912.

St Mary Street, *c.* 1893. The pillars of the Old Town Hall, opened in 1854, are to the left of the picture.

The Royal Hotel, St Mary Street, which was opened in 1866 is seen to the left of the picture, c. 1893.

Trams had taken over from the horse and cart in this St Mary Street picture taken around 1904.

Kingstone Court, *c*. 1902. There was a time when Cardiff town centre was cluttered with forty-five courts. These courts, which were open spaces between large buildings, included Thomas Court, Evans Court, Roberts Court, Jenkins Court, Dispensary Court, Landore Court, Mason's Arms Court, Kingstone Court, Green Garden Court, Kenton Court and Dalton Court.

Some, we are told, were neat and clean, while the condition of others was squalid. The entrance to these courts was often through a narrow and dark, forbidding passage. The courts were referred to in a government report of 1831, when the population of Cardiff was 6,137: 'The principal streets are paved and lighted and possess several respectable houses and shops. There are several courts, alleys and lanes behind the principal streets occupied by families bordering on pauperism, and a similar class of people is found even in some of the new streets, such as Charlotte Street, Caroline Street, and Irish Town and near the Canal.'

The report went on: 'Although the town is certainly thriving and likely to improve, it is appreciated that there will always be a shifty and pauper population in its suburbs in consequence of the description of labourers required for loading and discharging the vessels, for attending on the wharfs, and for other casual occupation.' How times have changed! The report went on to mention Milkmaid's Bridge. This was a stone bridge, which crossed the Glamorganshire Canal at the south end of the Hayes. It was called Milkmaid's Bridge because at one time cows crossed it to be milked. Also mentioned in the report was a reference to Love Lane, which is off Churchill Way, and which was said to have, at one time, stood to the left of a field called Eight Acres. How did Love Lane get its name? It is situated near what was at one time the notorious Mary Ann Street, where most of the town's prostitutes lived. Perhaps it was in Love Lane that the 'ladies of the night' touted for business.

Kingstone Court was situated between the Royal Arcade and Brains Brewery. The top of the Royal Hotel can be seen in the background, c. 1902.

These two workmen take a break to pose for this picture taken on the Site of Works department. Brains Brewery buildings are in the background.

Looking west, from the back of St Mary Street and to the rear of Andersons.

The back of St Mary Street,
c. 1902.

The residents of Green Garden
Court pose for this picture
taken around 1896.

Green Garden Court, *c.* 1928. Blackwell's bookshop is now situated on part of this site.

It's a pity that the young girl nursing the baby in a shawl to the right of the picture moved and spoiled this fascinating photograph of Kingstone Court, *c.* 1902.

Mr David Morgan, seen in the Tabernacle burial grounds, at The Hayes, *c*. 1902. The cemetery was later cemented over.

The corner of the Tabernacle burial grounds. Mr Percy Randle is standing in almost the same position as Mr David Morgan in the above picture. The picture was probably taken before the previous photograph, as telephone insulators can be seen on the wall in the top photograph.

Mr David Morgan posed for this picture, on 14 May 1898.

Rowes Square, The Hayes, c. 1890.

Landore Court was situated off St Mary's Street, near the Golate and the Queens Hotel, now the Irish Bank, *c.* 1880.

ones Court, situated off Womanby Street, has been preserved to some extent.

The Pallas Athene on the southern façade of the Old Central Library in Trinity Street.

Mayor Alfred Thomas declared the northern end of the Central Library open in 1882, while the southern extension was opened by the Prince of Wales, later King Edward Vll, in 1896. Cardiff was the first local authority in the Principality to adopt the Public Libraries Acts of 1850–55 and the old library served its patrons well for almost 100 years, until the new library on St David's Link was opened 1987. Working Street is on the right of the picture.

St David's Hall had not been built when this picture of Working Street was taken in the 1960s.

The former South Wales Electricity showrooms, in The Hayes, which adjoined the Glamorganshire Canal, began its life as 'The New Wholesale Fish, Poultry, Bird Game and Fruit and Vegetable Market' in 1901. It was built on the site of the old St John's infant school. These days the Abbey National Bank and Dillons bookshop are situated on the opposite side.

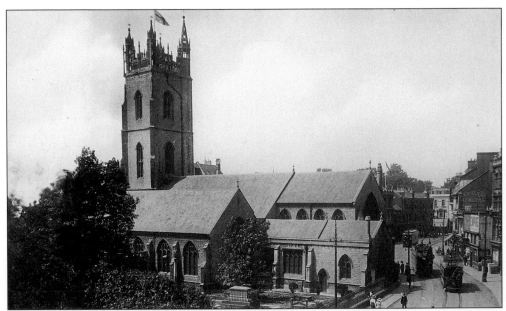

'St John's church is the most beautiful old church in the whole of South Wales. Its tall tower, with delicate perpendicular tracery, is a landmark from far away, but the church does not stand well for general inspection. The best way to view the church is to look down Church Street from St Mary Street. According to the old sixteenth-century map of Cardiff, the church of St Mary was at least twice as large as this church of St John, but since the destruction of old St Mary's, St John's church has become the premier church of the town.' (J. Kyrle Fletcher, *Cardiff Notes: Picturesque and Biographical*.) The St Mary's church that Kyrle Fletcher refers to was founded in the twelfth century, and stood near the south gate at the bottom end of St Mary Street near the River Taff. It was severely damaged in the great flood of January 1607, and by 1736 was no longer in use.

This engraving by J.H. Lekeux depicts the Town Hall in 1841, as viewed from the ruins of Cardiff Castle. St John's church tower to the left of the picture dominates the scene.

St John's church, c. 1850.

St John's church, c. 1950.

'The Grey Friars (Franciscans or Friars Minor) had their house in Crockherbtown, south of the new City Hall. After the dissolution, the site was acquired by Sir George Herbert, and his grandson, Sir William, built a mansion on the site, known as The Friars. A portion of this is still standing and is a light handsome structure in Tudor style. The site of the Grey Friars church was excavated by the Marquis of Bute, who had the outlines rebuilt to a few feet above the ground. Some graves inside the church were discovered and marked. It is known that Llewellin Bren and his foe, Sir William Fleming, were buried here, but attempts to identify the graves were not satisfactory.' (John Ballinger's *Guide to Cardiff*, published in 1908). Sadly the ruins of Herbert House were demolished in 1958, and the Pearl Assurance building now occupies this historic site.

Herbert House, Greyfriars. St John's school was built on the site of the churchyard, c. 1928.

This picture of Herbert House was taken in 1909.

Magnet House, Kingsway, c. 1955. To the extreme right of the picture can be seen the wall that was built to surround the ruins of Herbert House.

Magnet House has long since gone and this building on the same site today is known as Number 1 Kingsway. This picture was taken in 1998.

Kingsway, c. 1960.

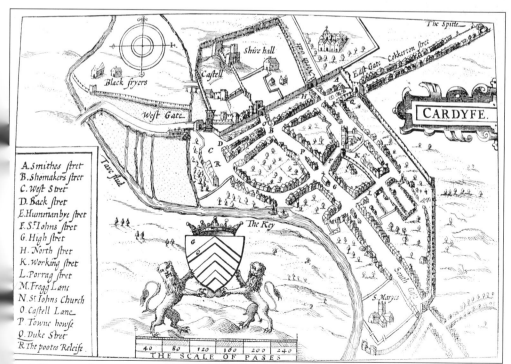

A. Smithes ſtret
B. Shomakers ſtret
C. Weſt Stret
D. Back ſtret
E. Hummanbye ſtret
F. St Iohns ſtret
G. High ſtret
H. North ſtret
K. Working ſtret
L. Porrag ſtret
M. Frogg Lane
N. St Iohns Church
O. Caſtell Lane
P. Towne howſe
Q. Duke Stret
R. The pootes Releife

Cardiff owes its beginnings to the path of the River Taff as can be seen by Speed's Map of 1610.

Cardiff Bridge, *c.* 1871.

CANTON BRIDGE, CARDIFF.

This postcard from the 1930s, refers to Cardiff Bridge as Canton Bridge, as it is sometime erroneously known.

Kingsway, looking north, *c.* 1900.

Cardiff Free Library, *c.* 1904. Working Street is to the right of the picture and St John's church on the left.

The junction of Duke Street and Queen Street. The Red Lion public house is on the corner of Kingsway and Queen Street. The banner is advertising the Cardiff Flower Show in the Drill Hall.

Wharton Street, *c.* 1936. The *Western Mail* and *South Wales Echo* were produced in th[...] building, from 1930. It is now known as Golate House, and continued to occupy the site f[...] over thirty years. In 1961, the newspapers moved to the new building in Havelock Street whic[...] was opened by Roy Thomson.

The headquarters of the Fire Brigade, stood in Westgate Street from 1917 until 1973. This is now the site of a multi-storey car park.

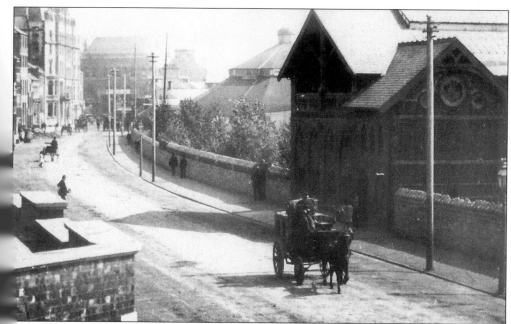

Westgate Street, c. 1880. The Hippodrome Theatre is behind the old Jackson Hall, while in the distance the Theatre Royal can be seen.

The Royal Hotel, St Mary Street, *c.* 1890.

The Royal Hotel, St Mary Street, *c.* 1990. These two pictures were taken from almost the same spot but around 100 years apart. In the top picture horses and carriages were the main source of transport as opposed to the present time when cars and buses rule the streets.

Westgate Street, looking towards Wood Street and Temperance Town, *c.* 1871.

he post office in Westgate Street was built on the site of Hutchinson's and Tayleur's Wooden
rcus Theatre, in 1896. The building has not been used for some time.

A sketch by Sam Allen of the Hayes Bridge Road, in 1859.

The statue of John Batchelor, the Friend of Freedom. John Batchelor was a public-spirited man who died in 1883. His statue, which has been moved on several occasions, was erected in 188 Solly Andrews' store and the infants school can be seen in the background.

East Canal Wharf, c. 1910.

Hills Terrace, c. 1950. The Glamorgan Canal ran under the bridge. Dillon's Bookstore and the Abbey National Bank are now situated near this spot.

Quay Street, which leads from the High Street to Westgate Street, *c.* 1891. St John's church is in the background.

The approach to the Taff Vale railway station which, these days, is better known as Queer Street station, *c.* 1890.

The first Queen Street Bridge, *c*. 1903.

The Taff Vale railway offices, on the corner of Queen Street and Station Terrace, were built in 1860 and demolished in 1973. The AA Insurance Building is now situated on this site.

Two views of Queen Street Bridge also known as Rhymney Bridge. The top picture was taken in 1975, and the bottom one was taken when it had been modernized, not long afterwards.

The above picture of Dumfries Place was taken in 1964 and the bottom one in 1975. All the offices were demolished to make way for a multi-storey car park.

Dumfries Place, after all the offices were knocked down, in 1978.

The Old Town Hall in St Mary's Street, *c*. 1915. This building replaced the Guildhall in High Street in 1853.

Evans Court in North Street was demolished in the late 1890s and is now part of Kingsway.

Trinity chapel in Womanby Street, c. 1880. This street was once known as Hundemanby Street which is thought to mean 'The home or dwelling of the houndman.'

Wood Street Congregational chapel, in 1971.

St David's church, Charles Street, was bombed during the Second World War and rebuilt after the war. It is now St David's Cathedral.

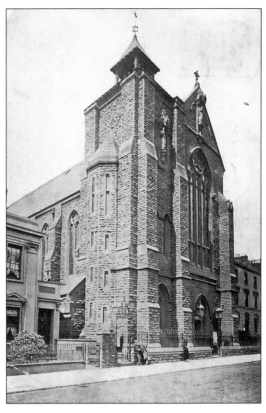

The Wesleyan chapel, Charles Street, in 1984.

Aberdare Hall, Cathays Park, *c*. 1908. The Jacobean style red brick and terracotta building opened as a hostel for women students.

The Glamorganshire and Monmouthshire Deaf and Dumb Mission at 25 Windsor Place wa closed in 1972.

McConnochie House, 20 Park Place, was designed by William Burgess, the architect for the Marquis of Bute, and was built around 1872. John McConnochie came to Cardiff from Scotland in 1855, and was appointed resident engineer to the Bute Docks. McConnochie House was later known as Park House.

The Guildford Crescent swimming baths were opened by the Lady Mayoress, Lady Windsor, in 1886. The baths, where thousands of Cardiffians learned to swim, were closed in 1984 and later demolished to make way for a car park.

King Edward VII hospital, on Newport Road and Glossop Road, was built in 1883, on the site of the Cardiff Tredegarville cycling track, where penny-farthing cycle races were held, *c*. 1913. Since 1923, it has been known as the Cardiff Royal Infirmary.

Cardiff Prison, on Knox Road, was opened in 1857, and replaced an earlier prison built in 1832. The last execution took place here in 1952, and this photograph was taken somewhat later, around 1960.

Four
Shops and Businesses

Anthonie in
High Street and
St Mary Street
was just one of
the many shops
sold by Messrs
Stephenson and
Alexander, the
old established
chartered
auctioneers and
estate agents
who operate
from the High
Street.

The entrance to the St Mary Street market is to the left of the picture. The decorated building was celebrating the wedding of the Marquis of Bute, and is called the Borough Arms.

An advertisement for a Christmas Market, in 1875.

BOROUGH OF CARDIFF.

CHRISTMAS MARKET.

NOTICE IS HEREBY GIVEN, that the CHRISTMAS MARKET will be held on FRIDAY, the 24th day of December instant.

Dated this 8th day of December, 1875.

DANIEL JONES.

MAYOR.

PRINTED AT THE "WESTERN MAIL" OFFICES, CARDIFF.

Anderson & Co., in St Mary Street billed themselves as 'The cheapest clothiers in the world,' *c.* 1890.

T.W. Long & Co., the jewellers, were situated at 2 St Mary Street, in 1909.

The wholesale cellars of R.P. Cully were located at 92 Queen Street, in 1909.

Charles Marment's was situated at 20–21 Duke Street, in 1910.

The Royal Arcade, *c*. 1920.

The Morgan Arcade was named after David Morgan, who started out in business with a gentlemen's outfitter's on The Hayes, in 1910.

The Royal Arcade is the oldest of Cardiff's arcades and dates back to around 1858.

High Street Arcade was opened between 1880 and 1887. It was designed to make it possible for shoppers to walk from High Street directly to St John's Square.

Duke Street Arcade, c. 1910. The arcade leads into High Street and St John's Square, and was built around 1902.

Dodds, the newsagents, at 31 Caroline Street. The young man on the left of the picture is Reg Condon, who worked in the newspaper trade all his life.

In 1909, a Gent's Roadster would have set you back ten guineas.

The Automobile Co.

of Cardiff, Limited,

20-22, CHARLES STREET,
CARDIFF.

AUTOMOBILES.

NAPIER,

GLADIATOR,

MINERVA,

BELSIZE.

GARAGE AND REPAIRS

DAY and NIGHT.

Nat. Tel., 814.

Telegrams:
"AUTOCAR, CARDIFF."

The Automobile Company was based in Charles Street, in 1909.

The man in the middle of this picture is Ben Johnson, a representative for F. Day & Co., the wholesale haberdashery and general merchant's in Bridge Street, c. 1930. The gentleman wearing a hat is thought to be Mr Day himself.

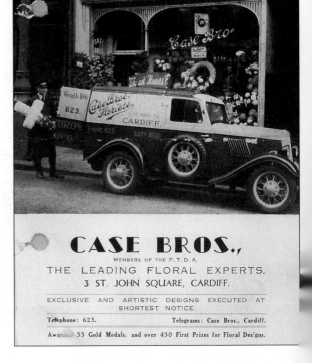

Case Brothers, the leading floral experts, at St John's Street. Around 1947, when this picture was taken, the cost of a wreath, as seen on the van door, was ten shillings and sixpence. St John's Street is popularly known as St John's Square.

Larkins, the wholesaler's, on Hills Terrace. Frederick Street is to the extreme left of picture, *c*. 1950.

Siemens & Brown Brothers Limited, on Hills Terrace. Frederick Street is on the extreme right of the picture, *c*. 1950.

Queens Street Arcade, taken from the Working Street entrance, in 1947. Mackross was a popular store in the late 1940s and 1950s.

Phillips and Co., were tea specialists, on Churchill Way, in 1956. Tandy's now occupies this site.

Hope Brothers, 1 St Mary Street, in 1967. This building, on the corner of Church Street and St Mary Street, was once the residence of a well-known landowner 'Squire' John Richards.

PLAN No. 2

CASTLE STREET		DUKE STREET
H. & S. Electricals		Burton (Tailors)
The Blue Bell (P.H.)		National Bank
A. Rose (Tailors)		
Jaeger (Fashion)		Cresta Silks (Fashion)
Hector Powe (Tailors)		W. H. Smith and Son
Thos. Cook & Sons		
Lloyds Bank / Welsh Sports		Anros (Fashion)
CASTLE ARCADE	HIGH STREET	Richard Henry (Hair Fashions)
Lotus (Footwear)		Maypole (Supermarket)
Bewlay (Tobacconists)		Mayfair Restaurant
		Watches of Switzerland
Phoenix Assurance Co. Ltd.		HIGH STREET ARCADE
Peter Lord (Footwear)		Courts (Furnishers)
National Fur Company		
ANTHONIE		Bungalow Cafe
		Olivers (Footwear)
QUAY STREET		CHURCH STREET
Trustee Savings Bank		
The Griffin (P.H.)		Hope Brothers (Outfitters)
National Provincial Bank	SAINT MARY STREET	T. W. Long & Co. (Jewellers)
Co-op Travel Service		Co-operative (Dept. Store)
Co-operative Wholesale Society		Stead and Simpson (Footwear)
		Cabot Fur Company
		Cardiff Market
C.W.S. Bank Ltd.		H. Samuel (Jeweller)
GUILDHALL PLACE		The Borough Arms (P.H.)
Barclays Bank Limited		James Howell and Co. Ltd.

plan of St Mary Street, in 1967.

William Lewis, the stationer's, occupied the corner of Queen Street and Charles Street when this picture was taken in 1965. Now it is a Burger King restaurant.

LOCATION PLAN

PARK LANE

JOHN TEMPLE *Men's Outfitters*

RADIO RENTALS
WILL SAM MOR *Paints*
JOHN CROUCH *Jewellers*
HENRY FIELDS *Skirt Shop*
DOLLAND & NEWCOMBE *Cameras*
VACANT
PENFOLDS SHOE SHOP
EVAN ROBERTS *Women's Fashion*

PARK PLACE

LEWIS SEPARATES *Women's Fashion*

SECCOMBES *Department Store*

WOODFORDS *Men's Outfitters*
SCHOLL *Shoe Shop*
COLERIDGE *Women's Fashion*
ARCADE
SODDENS *Women's Fashion*

TOM EVANS *Jewellers*
OLYMPIA CINEMA
SWEARS & WELLS *Women's Fashion*
MARSHALL *Women's Fashion*

ODEON CINEMA

DIXON *Cameras*

CALDER & SON *Gents Outfitters*

CHURCHILL WAY

NATIONAL PROVINCIAL BANK

WYMANS *Book Shop*

DUNN *Men's Outfitters*

LITTLEWOODS

THE CARD SHOP

DAVIS *Blankets Sheets etc.*

CHARLES STREET

MARKS & SPENCER

ENGLANDS *Shoe Shop*

PARADISE PLACE

TAFF VALE *Public House*

PALMER *Men's Outfitters*

PAIGE *Women's Fashion*

WESTONS *Women's Fashion*

MIDLAND BANK

F. W. WOOLWORTH

QUEEN STREET

N

A plan of Queen Street, in 1965.

90

The official opening of the extension to Littlewoods premises, in 1970. Staff look on as John Cargill (Littlewoods' office manager) holds the tape for Miss Backhouse (manageress) to cut.

The Littlewoods staff gather in Charles Street for the opening of the extension to the building in 1970. Sadly, the store closed, in 1998.

The Synagogue, in Windsor Place, in 1957. It is believed to have been built in 1870. Unfortunately, it was knocked down to make way for an office block which, in its turn, was being transformed into a restaurant in 1998. To the right of the picture is Austin Reed, the gentlemen's outfitter's, now taken over by Barclays Bank.

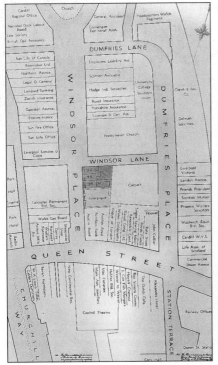

Left: A street plan of Windsor Place, in 1957. Right: Windsor Place, in 1964.

David Morgan, in The Hayes, in 1904. David Morgan commenced trading in 1879, at 23 The Hayes. The following year he took over the adjoining building on the south corner of Barry Lane. By 1884, he had become so successful that he had extended his business southwards along the Hayes and a five storey building was erected. Later, the acquisition of land between the rear of the Royal Arcade and Tabernacle Lane enabled him to increase the depth of the store. When George Hopkins's grocery store became available he acquired this too, and built a second five storey shop. The St Mary Street store was opened in 1898 and the following year the Morgan Arcade was completed.

David Morgan's premises after the first addition, in 1880.

Morgan Arcade, in St Ma[r]y Street, in 1902.

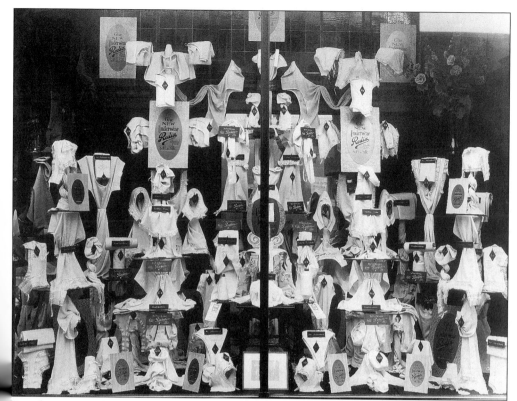

David Morgan, The Hayes, Redia underwear display window, *c.* 1926.

The counting house was situated on the first floor of the middle building. The Sumlock Comptometers were introduced to Great Britain, around 1926.

James Howell Arcade entrance, on Wharton Street, in 1925. 'There are few things in life you may be wanting or desiring that James Howell and Co. Ltd, cannot supply.' (*James Howell booklet*)

James Howell's staff posed for this picture, in 1925.

James Howell's grocery store, in Wharton Street. 'All the foods and spices you crave, gathered from the ends of the earth and the depths of the sea.' (*James Howell booklet*)

James Howell's motor garage, on Bakers Row, in Wharton Street. In 1925, James Howell could have provided you with a Rolls Royce, Austin, Citroën or Alvis, as well as a specially designed body for your present or new car.

James Howell customers, enjoying refreshment in the soda fountain, in 1925.

The old Central Library in Trinity Street is to the left of the picture which shows a merry-go-round. The Hayes Island Café is to the right, c. 1970.

Five

Leisure, Recreation and Sport

This 50hp Daimler could have been hired, 'at moderate rates', from Pidgeon's Hire Service in the 1930s.

The Empire Theatre, in Queen Street, in 1925.

In 1887, this building was opened as Levino's Hall and became the Empire Theatre in 1889. A C&A department store now occupies the site of this once famous theatre and cinema which closed as the Gaumont in 1960.

The Capitol Cinema, which opened in 1921, had a restaurant and dance hall. It closed on 21 January 1978.

The Capitol Cinema was knocked down to make way for the Capitol Exchange shopping complex, in 1983.

The Queens Cinema was known was the Picture Show in 1910, and was later called the Cardiff Cinema Theatre. In 1928, it has the distinction of being the first cinema in Cardiff to show 'talkies'. They presented *The Jazz Singer* which starred Al Jolson, the world's greatest entertainer.

The New Theatre, built by Messrs Runtz & Ford, was opened on the 10 December 1906. The productions staged were varied and included, music hall, drama, opera, variety and pantomime. You name it, the 'New' has staged it.

A poster advertising a concert held by the County Borough of Cardiff.

The Park Hall Cinema, c. 1962. The cinema was opened as a concert hall in 1885, and became a cinema in 1916. A certain Mr Winston Churchill once lectured there. The last films to be shown at this magnificent picture house were *Operation Crossbow* and *Seven Brides for Seven Brothers*. It was sadly demolished in 1980.

Cardiff's first purpose-built theatre, the Theatre Royal, was opened in 1826; it was built on part of the ground where the Park Hall had stood. Other early theatres were the wooden Circus Theatre in Westgate Street, built in 1876, and the 'new' Theatre Royal in St Mary Street, built in 1878. This theatre was re-named the Play House in 1920 and then the Prince of Wales Theatre in 1935. This pictute was taken around 1965.

The 'new' Theatre Royal, on St Mary Street and Wood Street, *c*. 1890.

The Pavilion in St Mary Street started life as the Philharmonic and was later called the Panoptican. It was converted to a bingo hall in 1970.

The Central Cinema on The Hayes was converted from a roller skating rink, in 1911. The cinema closed in 1959, and is now the site of the Oxford Arcade. Anna Kashfi worked in the butcher's shop, seen in the picture. She later became a Hollywood film actress and married Marlon Brando in 1957.

The author's maternal grandfather, Patrick Donovan, standing fifth from the left, was a member of the Ex-Servicemen's Club in Frederick Street, where he lived, *c.* 1946.

The Cardiff Comrades Club and Institute, in Paradise Place. The white building, which can just be seen at the end of the club, was the Taff Vale public house in Queen Street, *c.* 1967.

The Cowbridge Arms stood on the corner of Broad Street and Angel Street. Angel Street was a narrow street which ran parallel with Castle Street, and became part of Castle Street in 1884.

The Lifeboat Inn in Little Frederick Street was demolished in 1978, along with the Taff Vale public house.

A crowd gathers outside the Golden Cross public house, c. 1890. This pub started life as the Shields and Newcastle Tavern in 1849, and was then called the Castle Inn in 1855. It took its present name in 1863.

One of the oldest inns in Cardiff was the Angel Hotel, which dates back to 1666. It was moved to its present site in Castle Street after the demolition of the Cardiff Arms Hotel, in 1878.

The Masons Arms stood in Queen Street between 1795 and 1920. The site is now part of a shopping complex. This picture was taken around 1903.

In 1974, the Rose & Crown, in Kingsway, was demolished, despite a campaign to get it listed by the Welsh Office. The new public house built in its place was also called the Rose & Crown until it was renamed Coopers, in 1997.

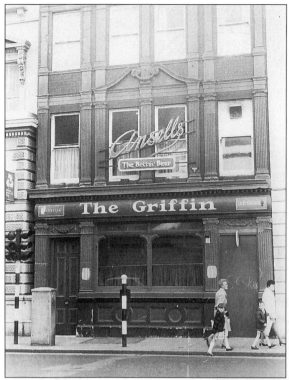

The Griffin, in Queen Street, was demolished in 1974, and is now part of the NatWest Bank. In earlier times, there used to be another public house of the same name on the other side of the road.

The Horse & Groom, in Womanby Street, dates back to at least 1835. It was the place for 'press-gangings' in earlier days and is said to be haunted by a poltergeist.

The British Volunteer Hotel, The Hayes,
c. 1890.

The Three Horse Shoes, stood in High
Street, from 1798 until 1913. It is now
the site of a building society. This picture
was taken around 1890.

Dutch Café, Cardiff

The Dutch Café in Queen Street, near the Taff Vale railway station, was a popular venue with thousands of Cardiffians for many years. Halfords took over the premises in 1950. The plaques of the Dutchmen on the front of the building were preserved when the building was demolished and have been incorporated into the brickwork of the new Capitol Exchange shopping centre, in Station Terrace.

These cold drinks and tasty snacks machines were installed at the Wales Empire swimming pool in the 1960s.

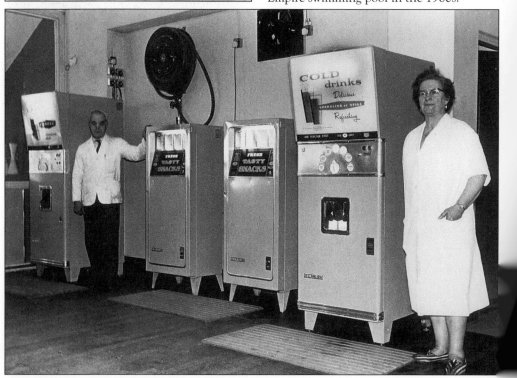

Victor Hall, who lived in Canal Street, worked at the Guildford swimming baths from 1934, and later at the Wales Empire swimming pool as manager, until his retirement in 1970. He was a Welsh water-polo player, and also competed in the Taff Swim when it was held at Roath Park Lake.

It may look like an open-air swimming baths, but this is a picture taken of the Cardiff Arms Park cricket pitch, now the Cardiff RFC ground, under water, in August 1963.

Taking the plunge at the Wales Empire swimming pool. The restaurant can be seen in the background, c. 1959.

The Olympic Games swimmer, Adrian Moorhouse, wearing the British Gas t-shirt, is pictured with these Cardiff youngsters at the Wales Empire swimming pool, in 1992.

In 1970, the length of the Wales Empire swimming pool had to be shortened to meet international standards. Roy Wedlake worked day and night for a week to complete the job and lost half a stone in the process.

Lifeguard, Brian Goodman, keeps a watchful eye over these youngsters enjoying themselves at the Wales Empire swimming pool, c. 1970.

The author, Brian Lee, then aged 45, competing in the 1981 *Western Mail* Marathon. He finished a respectable 135th in a huge field of more than 3,500 runners, clocking 3 hours 13 minutes 14 seconds. The course proved to be 700 yards too long and the race was won by Great Britain runner, Bernie Plain, from Cardiff, in 2 hours 26 minutes 04 seconds.

The competitors thread their way through Castle Street just after the start of the 1981 *Western Mail* Marathon.

The opening ceremony of the Sixth British Empire and Commonwealth Games at the Arms Park, in July 1958.

The Australian, Herb Elliott, seen on the outside of the leading three, was on his way to winning the mile. He won in a time of 3 mins and 59 secs and was never beaten at the distance during his athletic career.

The famous Cardiff Arms Park, as it was at the turn of the century. Many older readers will recall how daring fans of Welsh rugby would shin up the posts before international matches at the Arms Park, often to fix a leek as high as possible, while the crowd chanted, 'Up, up, up!' Often games were contested on a swamp land with mud inches deep because the pitch was used extensively as the home of Cardiff RFC. On the Sunday after the Wales v. South Africa monsoon match on 3 December 1960, the pitch was flooded to a depth of three feet when the Taff burst its banks.

In 1941, a German landmine destroyed the North Stand and river end terracing. J.C. Walker, the renowned cartoonist of the *Western Mail* and *South Wales Echo*, depicted an American viewing the devastation and being told the last game played there had been between Wales and England. 'Gee!' says the Yank, 'It sure must have been a helluva game!'

Eventually, Cardiff RFC moved next door to construct a new home on the cricket ground where Glamorgan had played so many matches when they won their first county championship in 1948. This became possible as Glamorgan developed their headquarters across the river at Sophia Gardens in 1967.

Wales, captained by John Dawes and with such luminaries as J.P.R. Williams, Barry John, Gareth Edwards, Mervyn Davies, Dai Morris and John Taylor, defeated a President's XV, scoring 26 – 11 in a match to celebrate the official opening of the redeveloped National Ground on 17 October 1970. The final match on the ground saw Cardiff win the SWALEC Cup 33 – 26, against Swansea on 26 April 1997. A crowd of only 39,000 witnessed the event because demolition work had already begun and the West Stand had been dismantled. And so, a world famous venue that had seen its first club fixture on 21 November 1874, and was named after The Cardiff Arms coaching inn which stood nearby, was no more. But its myriad memories will be with us forever. (John Billot, Former Sports Editor of *The Western Mail*)

Bill Hardiman, the ground manager for the Welsh Rugby Union, can be seen cutting through the snow on the Arms Park pitch, but the ground was unplayable after a blizzard and this meant the cancellation of the Barbarians *v.* Australia match on 9 January 1982.

The Welsh XV which defeated England 30–9, at Cardiff Arms Park to win the Triple Crown, in 1969. Standing, from left to right: D.P. d'Arcy (referee), S.J. Watkins, W.D. Thomas, T.M. Davies, B. Thomas, D. Williams, W.D. Morris, D.J. Lloyd, and F.B. Stephens (touch judge). Seated: D.C.T. Rowlands (coach), J.P.R. Williams, J. Young, G.O. Edwards (captain), K.S. Jarrett, and M.C.R. Richards. At the front: S.J. Dawes, J. Taylor, and B. John.

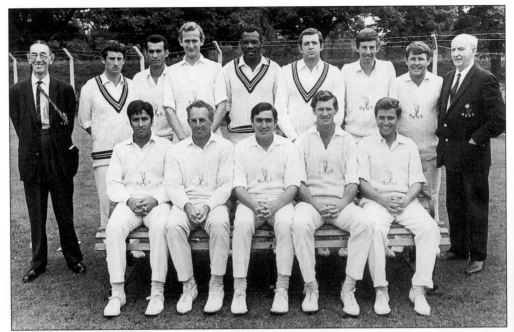

The Glamorgan County Cricket Champions of 1969. Standing, from left to right: Hugh Jeffreys (scorer), Kevin Lyons, Bryan Davis, Malcolm Nash, Tony Cordle, Lawrence Williams, Roger Davis, Eifion Jones, and John Evans (physiotherapist). Seated: Majid Khan, Don Shepherd, Tony Lewis (captain), Peter Walker, and Alan Jones.

These Littlewoods employees show off the Littlewoods Challenge Cup. They are, from left to right: Jill English, Lesley Bennett, Alison Wade, Sarah Cunningham and Miss Littlewood 198? Liza Barry. The Littlewoods store which closed in 1998 is seen left of the picture.

Six

Events

here follow extracts from a programme
ublished for a reception given in honour
f the British Antarctic Expedition, in
910, before Captain Scott and his men
et out on their ill-fated expedition.

CITY OF   CARDIFF.

BRITISH ANTARCTIC EXPEDITION, 1910.

—::—

RECEPTION

GIVEN BY

THE LORD MAYOR & THE LADY MAYORESS

(Alderman and Mrs. JOHN CHAPPELL),

AT

THE CITY HALL, CATHAYS PARK,
ON TUESDAY, 14TH JUNE, 1910, AT 8 P.M.,

TO MEET

CAPT. R. F. SCOTT, C.V.O., R.N., D.SC.,
AND OFFICERS OF THE ABOVE EXPEDITION.

—::—

PROGRAMME.

REFRESHMENTS will be provided in the Luncheon Room—
South Eastern Corridor.

MENU.

Tea, Coffee, Milk and Cream.

—

Fancy, White and Brown Bread and Butter.

—

Chicken, Tongue, Beef and Cucumber Sandwiches.

—

Fancy Strawberry, Orange, Vanilla, Apricot, Peach, and
Moccha Gateaux.

—

Fancy Petit Fours, Pedro, Venice, Eclairs, Operas, Crescents and
Almond Fingers, Macaroons, Paris Desserts, Readings,
Phillipine, Dessert and Wine Biscuits.

—

Cherry, Madeira, and Sultana Cakes.

—

Wine Jellies, Trifles, Strawberry Creams.

—

Claret Cup.   Iced Lemonade.   Orangeade.
Vanilla and Strawberry Cream Ices.
Wafers.

—

DESSERT.

This is a menu of the food served at the reception, given by the Lord Mayor, Alderman John Chappell and Lady Mayoress, Mrs M.A. Chappell.

PROGRAMME.

The following Selections will be rendered by
Madame HUGHES-THOMAS' ROYAL WELSH LADIES' CHOIR.

GLEES .. .. (a) "Nos Galan" ..		Arranged
(b) "Y Deryn Pur" ..		by
(c) "Clychau Aberdyfi"		Emlyn Evans
The Choir.		
SONG .. "O Peidiwch a dweyd wrth fy Nghariad"		
Miss Mari Edmunds.		
SONG & CHORUS .. .. "Killarney" ..Arr. by Hugh Hughes		
Miss Jennie Emmanuel and Choir.		
GLEES (a) "Let the Hills resound with Song" Brinley Richards		
(b) "Cydgan y Morwyr" ("The Sailors' Chorus") Parry		
The Choir.		
SONG .. .. "The fair hills of Erin".. .. Needham		
Miss Marianne Squire and Choir.		
SONG .. .. "My Ain Folk" .. .. Lemon		
Miss Nansi Langdon.		
GLEES .. (a) "Nyni yw'r Merched Cerddgar".. .. Gwent		
(b) "Wlad, hoff Wlad"		
The Choir.		
GLEES .. .. (a) "Ar hyd y Nos" .. Arranged by		
(b) "Llwyn Onn" .. Emlyn Evans		
The Choir.		
DUETT .. .. "The Venetian Boat Song" .. Blumenthal		
Misses M. Squire and Nansi Langdon.		
SONG .. .. "Merch y Melinydd"		
Miss Alice M. Lewis.		
GLEES .. (a) "Bugeilio'r Gwenith Gwyn"		
(b) "Hob y Deri Dando" Arr. by Prof. David Evans		
The Choir.		
MUSICAL JEST .. "An Italian Salad" .. .. Genee		
Miss Marianne Squire and Choir.		
TRIO .. "Rest thee on this mossy pillow" .. Smart		
Misses Beatrice Langford, Mabel Scott, and Flossie Bowen.		
GLEES .. ... (a) "Welsh Rhapsody" .. .. Vincent		
(b) "Song of the Sailors" .. Minara		
(c) "Night Hymn at Sea" .. Thompson		
The Choir.		
"HEN WLAD FY NHADAU."		
"DUW CADW'R BRENIN."		

Madame Hughes-Thomas' Royal Welsh Ladies' Choir offered a musical accompaniment to the evening, singing a mixture of Welsh and English tunes.

This is the picture of Captain R.F. Scott, as he appeared in the programme.

Lieutenant E.R.G.R. Evans, whose picture also appeared in the programme.

Bunting was strung up in the city centre in celebration of the wedding of the Marquis of Bute, in 1872.

The Marquis of Bute's statue is shown at its original location, in High Street.

The city centre, as it was decorated for
Queen Victoria's Jubilee.

The citizens of Cardiff gathered outside the offices of the *Western Mail* and the *South Wales Daily News* in St Mary Street on Election Day for news of the results, in 1892.

In 1900, Ivor Novello celebrated his seventh birthday and was taken by his mother, Madame Clara Novello, to Mr J. Osborne Long's photographic studios at 62 Queen Street to have this portrait taken. He later became a famous composer, film star and matinée idol. He died in 1951.

Ivor Novello was born at 95 Cowbridge Road East, a little further along the road from where this picture was taken in the 1900s.

The Novellos later moved just around the corner to 11 Cathedral Road, as seen in this picture.

andaff Fields, where the young Ivor Novello would have played, is at the end of Cathedral
ad and was opened to the public, in 1898.

Brian Lee with his first book in the *Archive Photographs* Series *Cardiff Remembered*.

Acknowledgements

First of all I would like to thank the editors of the *South Wales Echo* and *Cardiff Post*, for publishing my requests to readers for photographs of Cardiff. Without their help it is doubtful whether this book would have appeared.

Special thanks go to Matthew Williams, Curator at Cardiff Castle, for writing the introduction and to John Billot, former sports editor of the *Western Mail*, who wrote the piece on the Cardiff Arms Park, as well as providing me with some of the pictures that are seen with it. I am grateful to the staff of Cardiff Central Library, Local Studies Department for their help, and especially to J. Brynmor Jones who has proved a valued friend over the years.

For the loan of photographs, and permission to use them, I am greatly indebted to the following people: David Davies; FRICS of Stephenson & Alexander, High Street, Cardiff, one of the oldest firms of surveyors operating in the principality today; fellow author, Geoff North; Maureen and Fred MacCormac; Anne Dickson; Mrs A. Hobbs; Mary and Philip Donovan; Mr Phyllis Condon; Idris John; Bill Penny; Irene Godfrey; Peter Narusberg; Peter Persen; Leslie Hawer; Andrew Davies; Tony Lebeau; Phil Street; George Frantzeskou of Cardiff County Council's Leisure and Sports Section; Denis Pope of Pope's Photo Service, Canton; Cardiff Central Library; Western Mail & Echo Limited; John Morgan of David Morgan Ltd; and Marilyn McLucas of James Howell Ltd.

Many thanks to Maureen and Fred MacCormac for typing the typescript and captions.

I would also like to thank those people who offered photographs which, for one reason or another, were not used and ask forgiveness of any contributors who may have been inadvertently omitted from these acknowledgements.